Addition

"George Taylor's clear step-by-step guidebook to a more fulfilling relationship is both wise and full of heart."
–James Baraz, author of *Awakening Joy*

"In this book, George Taylor beautifully lays out a path to a very different kind of relationship: one of authentic communication and true connection."
–Sharon Salzberg, author of *Lovingkindness*, and *Real Happiness*

"*A Path for Couples* is the most useful book for couples I've seen. George Taylor bolsters his three decades of personal and professional experience working with couples with important empirical evidence from positive psychology and neurobiological research. The result is a set of skillful practices which help couples feel connected, joyful and relaxed."
–Christine Carter, author of *The Sweet Spot*

A Path
for
Couples

Ten Practices
for
Love and Joy

A PATH
FOR
COUPLES

TEN PRACTICES
FOR
LOVE AND JOY

GEORGE TAYLOR, MFT

Smuggling Donkeys Press
100 Toyon Dr., Fairfax CA 94930

Cover design, photo edit & interior layout: Lesley Thornton-Raymond
Cover image: created by Marc Takaha and Jason Miller
Back cover photograph: by Margot Duane
About the Author photograph: Margot Duane
Art direction: Katherine Dieter

ISBN: 978-0-9644129-1-0
Printed in the USA on acid free paper
10 9 8 7 6 5 4 3 2

Table of Contents

Introduction

After just four sessions using the Practices in *A Path for Couples,* a couple came into my office talking about the positive changes in their relationship.

"I don't know what you did, but it worked," Jack, a doctor at a prestigious medical center, said. "I feel so much closer to Sally."

Sally smiled. Her body language, which had been reserved and tense in the first two sessions, had softened. "Yes. Something big has shifted in our relationship. Jack isn't as mad, and I'm not walking on eggshells. These old patterns and conflicts are easier to manage."

"And?" I asked her. Sally, a forty-year-old nurse practitioner, had a tendency to see the glass as half full.

"Okay," she laughed. "I feel so much more at ease. It is easier to talk to him, and of course that leads to connection. Our kids noticed it too. They are so much better behaved."

"It's not magic," Jack added. "I feel safer now that Sally isn't going to snipe at me, or undercut me. Of course, I have to stop provoking her, as well."

"That sounds good," Sally laughed again. "We've been doing the Ten Practices at home. And we can talk about things, and reach decisions without blowing up."

"Even the remodel." Jack laughed. "Who knew?"

Every couple that uses the Ten Practices will not have such a positive response, but it's common for me to hear stories of couples making great changes quickly, whether it's those I have in counseling, or those who use these practices at home.

Sally and Jack were perfect candidates for *A Path for Couples,* even though they both had demanding jobs, and parented two children, ages eight and ten.

They have a committed relationship. And they know that they have to look into themselves if they expect change to come to their communications.

When Sally said that she is no longer "walking on eggshells," she was noting an important truth in her relationship. She was afraid to become vulnerable to Jack. Probably she had learned to protect herself in other relationships or as a child, so she had brought some bad habits and painful beliefs to her current relationship, like all of us do.

Jack became aware that when he moved toward Sally, he sometimes felt angry with her. That's what Sally felt, his anger. As Jack learned to describe his desire to connect with her, Sally could feel his warmth.

Sally and Jack needed instruction on how to be truly vulnerable to each other. I have been working with couples like Sally and Jack for twenty-five years. The Ten Practices they are using are designed to help couples create:

- More joy and love
- Less conflict and fewer power struggles
- More intimacy
- More creativity and collaboration

Like a lot of couples, Jack and Sally had a few topics or patterns that regularly caused stress, and which had been repeated over and over in their long relationship. So it makes sense that they need a disciplined, regular method to examine these habits and to change them.

Some couples will have immediate results, like Sally and Jack. Others will take longer. But I can offer a couple of guarantees. If you don't look at yourself and your own reactions, the regular conflicts you get into with your partner will persist. The pain and distance you and your partner create will persist.

If you regularly (once a week) do the Practices in this book, you will feel safer, happier and more creative in your relationship.
After a couple of more months with Sally and Jack, they were doing the Ten Practices regularly at home, and our sessions were less frequent.

"I can sense that we've just started the healing you have described," Sally said during one meeting. "I feel Jack's intention: to be on my side, to be my partner. What a relief."

And Jack spoke very softly, unlike his usual forceful presentation.

"There is a gift that Sally gives me every day, her love. I can feel how that opens up something deep inside me, something that was always there. Something like kindness or peace, or ease."

Sally looked lovingly at Jack.

"With you, I can learn how to love."

The Ten Practices that Sally and Jack are learning have been created using powerful ideas about relationship, mindfulness and consciousness, which have only recently begun to permeate Western culture. Eastern disciplines like meditation have taught us how we can train our minds to become more compassionate and aware.

Key ideas from these disciplines have been adapted to models of relationship with the idea that you and your partner can transform your partnership into a path of healing and awareness.

These ideas are becoming more popular. Why?

When you begin to work on your relationship using this powerful new model, you experience more love, joy and vitality.

This book describes a series of ten simple exercises for couples. Besides adapting powerful meditation and consciousness tools to relationship healing, the Practices utilize the latest research in positive psychology and trauma work.

The Practices were inspired by the thousands of couples I have met in the twenty-five years of my professional career. Couples like Jack and Sally. Maybe couples like you and your partner.

You lead a busy twenty-first-century life. You are in a committed relationship. You might be parents. You probably work for a living. You maintain stable lives for your family.

Because of your own self-understanding, you have noticed that you have certain predictable patterns of behavior with your partner when you are stressed or anxious. These patterns can persist in a relationship for years or decades.

You understand that the path of love and awareness can help you transform these old patterns.

Important writers and teachers such as John Welwood, Stephen and Ondrea Levine, and Gay and Katie Hendricks have written about how the path of conscious relationship can also open us to deep knowledge of ourselves, to the greatness of the human heart, and to the mysterious feelings of connection and creativity, which we can experience with our partner. These feelings are the source of tremendous healing and liberation.

My wife, Debra, and I have been followers of this path since 1979. We were young when we met, and like many couples, we needed help to survive and to thrive. So we pursued a path of awareness, and we immediately became more aware of our own reactions and patterns. Knowing we needed to change these bad habits, we developed the Ten Practices and have done each of them many times.

We have learned that love and mindfulness can carry us on a vast river of healing, beyond our habits and expectations, and into powerful states of joy and consciousness.

In this way, we are not so different from other people who pursue a path of liberation, people maybe like you, who believe that you can become more loving and creative with your partner.

But in your day-to-day lives, you often become so busy with mundane errands that you rarely connect deeply. There is a hunger in your soul, which can be assuaged.

The Ten Practices in this book lead to freedom. Not just the freedom from bad communication habits we learned as children, but the freedom to blossom into your full capacities as adults, loving, powerful, and wise.

You can experience the vastness of love and forgiveness that are possible in your relationship. You become more compassionate and wise. You can see your partner as disciplined and able to become more loving and aware.

On this path, you unleash your natural creativity, power, and positive energy in communion with your beloved partner.

What a great life calls to you!

All client names have been changed to protect privacy.

CHAPTER ONE: HOW THE TEN PRACTICES CAN TRANSFORM YOUR RELATIONSHIP

Jeffrey and Tina had married in their forties, after both had success in their businesses and many short-term relationships. Their story illustrates some important principles about how couples who originally feel so close can with time create a sad level of distance.

Jeffrey's main complaint was that he felt unheard. In their second session with me, he said to Tina, "I never wanted this new bathroom. I feel so disconnected from the project, and from you."

She said, "I'll pay for it."

He said, "I still don't want it."

She looked at me with pure frustration and a look that said, "See what I have to put up with?"

"Did I ever say I wanted the new bathroom?" Jeffrey asked. He too looked angry.

She replied, "You never said you didn't. You posed objections every time I suggested something."

The tension in the room was escalating. I could see immediately how the project ground to a halt.

Tina greatly wanted to feel that they could work together in their marriage, and she was very frustrated that Jeffrey wouldn't play ball with her. But she was so used to being in charge that she didn't know how to create as equal partners, as husband and wife.

Jeffrey felt pushed around, unheard. What was his role in the ongoing conflict? He had never learned to voice his desires or his needs because he had been trained by a very argumentative father to shut up and listen.

This couple's struggle (and its resolution, which is described in the next section, "The Promise of Healing") shows how painful distance between partners arises.

We all create tension in our relationships, through mostly unconscious behaviors. This anxiety creates distance, and then the painful patterns of conflict start.

The tension between you and your partner manifests itself in many ways:

- You cannot finish a conversation without a fight or an interruption.
- One of you shuts down and withdraws when conflict starts.
- One of you escalates into anger when your partner disagrees with you.
- Conversations often devolve into painful repetitions of blame and defense.
- There is a sad dearth of cooperation, connection, and intimacy in day-to-day life.

Even couples who have begun to study themselves and their reactions can get caught up in repetitive conflicts, often when they begin to talk about specific difficult topics. The distance is painful and it makes them feel lonely and frustrated. **And perhaps worst of all, each partner can eventually feel powerless to create the kind of love and intimacy that they dream of.**

These predictable conflicts share a few basic characteristics:

- The conflicts can be repetitive and intractable (without some intervention or inquiry, such as the Ten Practices.)
- Each partner thinks that the other person needs to change.
- Most of the conflicts begin with deep feelings of anxiety in our body, which are hard to recognize and to describe.
- Because we don't recognize the anxiety as our own, we blame it on our partner.
- At the end of these conflicts, we may feel right or justified in our actions, but sadly we feel separate from our partner.

Eventually couples like you will understand a key principle in this work: **In any conflicted pattern that a couple repeats over and over, each person is somehow creating it.**

You may not know how you are unconsciously perpetuating the patterned conflict. The practices in this book will help you to understand this key point.

Unless you take this approach, which is called self-responsibility, your feelings of loneliness and resentment can begin to permeate other conversations. Then you and your partner experience more emotional volatility or distance.

These symptoms of fear arise from powerful questions that we are not aware of, like: Am I loved? Am I cared for? Will I be alone?

When you work with the communication model in this book, you will realize that in the conversations that predictably cause stress, it's not the topic itself that causes the problem. For Tina and Jeffrey, it's not the size or cost of the bathroom.

The repetitive fights are about communication, about being heard, about who has control, and about who is right and who is wrong, not about which mirror to pick.

The Ten Practices direct each person's awareness inward, towards themselves, so they can see how they might be unconsciously creating the repetitive conflicted conversation.

This awareness changes the dynamic of conflict completely.

When you start to see how your behavior and your beliefs contribute to the problem, change can occur.

If you keep blaming your partner, you cannot change the inner part of yourself that needs love and attention.

But if you take up the challenge of healing yourself, through love and awareness and through the practices in this book, great changes can occur.

The Promise of Healing: Why You Need the Ten Practices

When you realize that you want to transform your relationship, you have a vision of healing. You look for help because you want to let go of negative feelings, towards your partner and yourself.

You may feel that there is more love, creativity, joy, and enthusiasm inside you. You want to restore the experience of joy and connection you felt earlier in the relationship, but these positive feelings are blocked.

The Ten Practices enable you:
- To utilize mindfulness in your relationship. (Yes, you!)
- To learn a new way to communicate and to resolve conflicts
- To create powerful goals and intentions for the relationship
- To create new methods of collaboration which lead to joy

The Ten Practices provide a powerful path to generate more intimacy, more creativity, more warmth, and more happiness in your relationship.

The continuing story of Jeffrey and Tina and their bathroom

remodeling illustrates the promise of healing. The first sessions I described above ended in tension, with both of them stuck in their accusations and defenses.

In later sessions with them, I continued to reiterate the self-responsibility model and to focus on new communication skills.

In truth, I wasn't feeling hopeful about their ability to see their own roles in the struggle. Blaming and withdrawal continued for several sessions. I had forgotten about the power of the Ten Practices, which they were working on at home.

A month later, we were back on the same topic.

Tina said, "You know, we talked about the remodel at home a few times. I started trying to listen to Jeffrey, instead of out-arguing him."

"I think listening is mentioned in your book," Jeffrey laughed. "Being heard was a new experience for me."

The tone of their dialogue had softened quite a bit.

Tina continued, "I kept thinking about how our patterns provoke and stimulate each other. Everything I tried got us into this mess where we couldn't even talk about the bathroom. If I could just convince Jeffrey that I was right..."

"That never worked out so well," Jeffrey interjected and they both laughed.

"Right."

Jeffrey and Tina were leaning towards each other and smiling occasionally. The feeling in the room remained soft and connected. They had moved to self-inquiry from blame and accusation.

Jeffrey said, "I knew I'd have to be involved in the remodel, even though Tina said she'd deal with it. It's my house too and I've done a lot of construction. I'd be checking up on the contractors..."

"He couldn't let go of control," Tina laughed. I looked at her.

"Maybe I have the same problem," she added and laughed again.

"What changed for you, Jeffrey?" I asked.

Jeffrey continued, "I was so critical of Tina. After we used the Ten Practices at home, I realized how her controlling father had forced her to be independent and to fight back. I learned so much about her."

He reached out and touched her hand. "Tina didn't ever mean me any harm. Once I felt less afraid of her, we could talk openly, I found I was less attached to what I thought was so important—the color of the tile. I was so attached because I felt so powerless. And me opening up to tell her what I wanted was a big shift for me."

Tina said, "We both wanted to keep the connection alive, not cause more conflict. Jeffrey likes design. I want him to enjoy the process. I cannot just say to him, "This is how we will do it.""

"If I don't speak up," Jeffrey said. "I become obstructive and negative."

When a couple moves into self-reflection, as Jeffrey and Tina did in this meeting, they began to experience more vitality and positive energy.

Tina and Jeffrey are communicating openly and honestly now. While using the Ten Practices at home, they realized that their patterns of control and resistance began in childhood situations or in other relationships.

I tell couples this important concept over and over. Of course, you need to resolve the content issue that seems to be so important. The bathroom does need tile! But the emotional heat and stress is coming from your conditioning and beliefs.

The content always points towards a stuck pattern of communication that causes predictable tension. Focusing on the content, instead of the underlying feelings and patterns, actually prevents positive energy from flowing into the relationship.

A couple of weeks later, Jeffrey and Tina came in laughing.

"What?" I asked, when they sat down.

"We're going to Europe," Tina announced. "Yeah, we can connect there, rather than in the bathroom."

"We decided to wait on the remodel," Jeffrey said.

"After all that, it's funny," Tina said. "But really, the Ten Practices showed us the pattern of conflict we were in. That knowledge is worth the price of admission. I can see how many times I operate in the same exact way."

Tina looked fondly at Jeffrey. "What I wanted was to feel really connected to Jeffrey, and I thought a home project would do that. But it was just a symbol."

"What a relief," Jeffrey said. "No more plans, no more meetings with contractors. I got my life back."

"I just said the hell with the remodel. I want to go to France and make love," Tina said.

"When I finally said what I wanted, I had to quit being so pouty and be brave," Jeffrey chimed in. "I had to be strong." He looked at Tina. "You helped me with that."

"And I thought you were sexy," Tina continued. "It's going to be so easy to practice collaborating on smaller things now."

"Like taking out the garbage," Jeffrey laughed again.

"That's your job," Tina said, and she laughed as well.

Couples like Tina and Jeffrey will have their issues arise, in certain patterns and on certain topics, as I have said. (My wife and I have proved this rule for thirty-five years!)

But Tina and Jeffrey's story shows how the conversation about the patterns and conflicts can change dramatically, and lead to connection instead of separation. That growth and healing is the promise of the Ten Practices.

With a tuneup in your communication strategies, and with clear intentions for dialogue, most couples like you can make significant changes. You can move from protection to connection, from anger to understanding.

Moreover, you can learn how to turn mutual decisions into opportunities for growth, connection, and even fun.

You can feel alive, powerful and creative—together!

One key idea bears repeating. Tina and Jeffrey are beginning to realize how their stressful and conflicted patterns interconnect. This fact is true for most couples.

Your unconscious communications tend to stimulate reactive behaviors in your partner. This stimulus leads to the repetition and to the predictability I have described. You tend to do the same thing when you are provoked in a certain way, for example, when you are judged or accused.

It is not easy for some of you to identify these interlocking patterns, so here are some tips.

After a massive study of my own unconsciousness, and that of my many students, I have noticed that most patterns contain one or both of these two core interactions: the **attack-defend pattern** and the **pursue-withdraw pattern.**

Attacks almost always contain a judgment or a criticism, and evoke a defense of some kind. In a pursuit pattern, you move toward your partner in an attempt to connect, and for some reason your partner retreats. There are many variations on these patterns, and listed here.

Teacher-Student (one of you holds the position of being right)
Committed One-Uncommitted One (a variation of pursuer-withdrawer)
Over-responsible/Under-responsible Partners
Parent-Child
Dominator-Victim/Martyr
Caretaker-Needy One

If you think about these patterns, each position in the pair requires the other. Key questions to change the pattern are:

How did I learn my role in the pattern?
What do I get out of my role? (Usually protection.)

These are only samples of possible painful interactions with your partner. Often clients ask me, "How can I identify these patterns?" Here are some clues:

- Which one of you gets angry? When? How does the anger arise? What does your partner do in response?
- Is one of you often late or forgetful? What does the partner do in response?
- Are agreements between you clear? Is there a pattern of broken or confused agreements?
- What happens when one or both of you is tired, late, hungry, or overworked? Do specific patterns of tension arise?
- What kind of stressful conversations do you have about addictive processes? (Alcohol, other drugs, work, internet use, or pornography, to mention a few possibilities.)

You can name your unique variations of these patterns as you work with them. When you bring consciousness to the usual stressors in your relationship, you can change your habitual responses.

As you pay attention to your body signals, you open to the information that your body gives you. And this attention is a key to finding joy and bliss.

A Sad Failure to Connect: Why Couples Don't Make It

Couples who come to me for counseling usually say, "We have communication problems." The lively vitality and happiness they once shared, like Elvis, has left the room. Here is an example of one of these couples.

Julie and Danny told me their story at their first meeting with me. Their twenty-year-old son, Johnnie, was in jail for his second driving-under-the-influence charge while he was home for the summer from a prestigious college. Julie brought the unwilling Danny with her. Both were in their mid-forties.

"If we cannot communicate, then how can we parent well? And Johnnie has grown up with the distance we have created and our confusion about how to parent him." Julie began speaking, and she looked angrily at Danny.

"Okay," I said.

So far so good, I'm thinking. There is a basic level of awareness here. Some couples have no understanding of how the parents' relationship affects their kids.

"It's the way you are with him, both allowing and overbearing at the same time," she said.

Danny weighed in, "It feels hopeless. We cannot talk about this. I am more permissive, more accepting. Julie just bosses and never listens to me or Johnnie."

Julie seemed depressed and reserved with an angry edge.

Danny and Julie's accusations typify many couples' conflicts. I start to explain the need for vulnerable communication.

Julie said, "I feel so distant, I don't know if we can recover. I don't see any point in being vulnerable."

"You never are," Danny interrupted.

Later in the same session, Danny said, "I don't want to say demeaning things to you. I want to protect you, but then I feel resentful."

"You protect me? I protect you," Julie said. "You never protect me. You throw me under the bus."

Julie folded herself into her chair and crossed her arms.

"The goal here is to say things we've never said before," I reminded them calmly. My stomach has tied itself in knots listening to them. "You can talk like this at home. We need to establish some ground rules."

Julie looked at me, "When he shares, I feel more distant. More hopeless. If he cannot learn to change, how will we get through this?"

"By working on the communication model with me," I replied. "By using the Ten Practices."

"He cannot learn."

"She'll never admit that she has to change," Danny added.

They left, sullen and separate. Later, Julie called me to say that they cannot continue therapy.

"You just don't get it about how challenging Danny can be," she said.

Sadly, this couple has the insight to know that they are in trouble, that they are stuck in patterns. But they won't get help.

Why not? I've thought a lot about this. Here are the chief reasons:

- Couples like Julie and Danny get used to distance and don't know how to create a positive mood. They cannot let down their defenses and feel warm and vulnerable. Maybe as children they only felt emotional connections that were painful.

- Either or both partners are so mad or hurt that they feel helpless to open up. They don't have the skills they need, and don't feel that they can learn them.

- There is an old hurt that needs attention and is causing painful patterns, either in the relationship or from each person's childhood. The repetition of their predictable conflicted patterns seems unchangeable.

- People like Julie and Danny would have to look at how they are failing the relationship and not living up to their ideals of love and openness. Most of us have a hard time being that vulnerable and open, admitting our own mistakes. How easy it is to see our partner's flaws!

- For people like Julie and Danny, a kind of hopelessness or helplessness sets in. Neither partner feels that they or the other can change. This is an unrecognized form of depression.

Many of these couples will experience some friendship, generosity, thoughtfulness, and cooperation around the house. They will responsibly parent their children.

But many couples like Danny and Julie will remain tangled in their struggles for many years. This failure to heal will blight their emotional lives, and their children will feel the impact. **They will not feel the profound joy of both loving and of being loved deeply.**

Who Will Benefit from the Ten Practices?

This book is designed for people who have an interest in inner work, in personal growth. Many of you see your relationship as a powerful vehicle for transformation. Here are some other characteristics I have noticed.

- You and your partner have very busy lives with work, aging parents, house management, sometimes children, volunteering, and other projects. You invest your life energy in many different places.
- You want to spend more time on your relationship, but it is hard to schedule.
- You know that you have brought into your relationship both habits you learned as a child, and conditioning caused by painful experiences in previous relationships. These habits and experiences affect the way you react to your partner.
- You know that inquiry, meditation, and other practices that encourage self-knowledge and introspection can help you feel better about yourself and your relationship.
- You understand that this studying of yourself leads to positive changes in your relationship:
- You desire better communication, which leads to greater love and intimacy.
- You seek more patience and compassion in difficult conversations.
- You want a feeling of ease, peace, and connection.
- You believe that working on yourself with your partner can make you a more caring person.

I have good news for you.

The Ten Practices laid out here are a way of maintaining the garden of your relationship. You know by now that there are no quick fixes for deeply ingrained communication habits and relationship beliefs. But when you take the time to weed out the problems and create the future through planning and regular maintenance, great results occur.

The Ten Practices are simple activities that can help you transform your relationship. You can do them on your own schedule at home.

Most couples that I have worked with, who practice these skills for a half an hour a week for three months, have found the results described here. You can transform suffering and bad habits into opportunities for consciousness, love, and connection.

Couples on the path of transformation can create a powerful team, focused on healing and on bringing more love and awareness into the world.

How can this happen?

When you and your partner work on this program together, you become allies in the deepest sense of the word. You help each other learn how to become more loving. You turn predictable conflicts that you might have been experiencing for years into opportunities for healing and for consciousness.

When you feel this change, you feel good about yourself and your partner.

Intimacy, sensuality, and creativity can be reborn in the relationship, as if you have found again that wealth of good feeling and hope that characterized the "honeymoon" phase. You can get that feeling back!

Chapter 2: Essential Tasks for Couples

As I have worked with couples for the last twenty-five years, I created a set of practices for them. The practices are organized so that you develop a set of important relational skills as you work through them. And you can take confidence from the fact that these practices have been tested on thousands of couples who are looking for healing and growth.

The practices also address specific problems or opportunities in relationships. In Appendix 4, you will find a list of common relationship problems, and the best practice to use to address them.

Here are the essential tasks a couple must be able to accomplish
- Practicing Mindfulness
- Learning Authentic Communication
- Three Basic Skills: Self-Awareness, Self-Inquiry and Self-Disclosure
- Working with Intentions
    Seven Key Intentions
- Couple's Creativity or Frequent Power Struggles? It's Your Choice
- Bringing Consciousness to Power Struggles
    Predictable Patterns
- Creating Positive Conditions for Success and Collaboration

Practicing Mindfulness

Mindfulness is all the rage these days. You can find trainings in mindful eating, mindful dog walking, mindful car repairs, and much more. But why is mindfulness becoming so popular in our culture, and how can it be used in your relationship?

These are key questions we need to answer, because mindfulness is the most important task you need to accomplish, to have a healing, growth-oriented relationship. Mindfulness implies paying close attention to the actual occurrences around you, or inside of you. It is the opposite of multi-tasking.

The Ten Practices are based on mindfulness, which means being present with yourself, your partner, your friends and colleagues.

As I use the word in this book, mindfulness means carefully watching your own reactions to relationship interactions, communications and stressors. Another word for mindfulness is *awareness*. Without awareness of your reactions and communication patterns, I don't believe you can change them.

If we begin to pay attention to our breath, if we can keep our focus inside our bodies, we can begin to detect the small changes in our breathing that can be signals our body is giving us about our relationship. (Or maybe we just went up some stairs!)

In a conversation with our partner, this tightness of the breath is often a signal of fear, of separation. When we sense these feelings in our relationship, often a cascading set of other feelings and body sensations start to occur.

For example, we might get angry, to prevent anyone from knowing we are afraid. We might cry when we actually feel angry. Sometimes we make up a story about our partner; this is known as *projection.*

This set of cascading feelings and mental activity is what I call a *pattern*. Most couples have a few interacting patterns which cause most of the struggle or separation in the relationship. Without awareness of the breath and awareness of the body, we can create these patterns over and over, for decades.

Mindfulness is the doorway to changing our conditioned responses to our partner's behavior. Once we see our own behavior, we can begin to make better choices.

The good news about mindfulness is that most people can learn it. Mindfulness is an inherent skill of our senses and of our mind.

When we conduct our relationships with more awareness, we create more positive feelings: of joy, of love, of intimacy and of awareness.

Learning Authentic Communication

Learning authentic communication is a beginning step in healing the distance that has crept into your relationship. Many books talk about the need for open, vulnerable conversations, but they don't describe how you can learn the skills that you need to have them, as this book does.

You might have been hurt or abandoned in relationships, either present or past, so you can experience anxiety about being close.

Without knowing it, you often project that anxiety onto your partner, and you think, "If only my partner would change, I wouldn't feel this way."

Because I have seen so many couples with these hidden fears of intimacy, the Ten Practices begin by establishing trust and safety. A key learning here is new and effective communication habits. Let's start with an example of how these skills can be utilized.

Last year a couple that was contemplating divorce called me. The woman, Lorraine, said a couple of times on the phone, "We just don't have the tools to communicate clearly and to resolve problems. He uses his family against me, and we are not on the same page. We say the same things to each other over and over. Things used to be great, but not anymore."

Like many people who call me, Lorraine had identified a repetitive pattern in her relationship that causes considerable stress and conflict.

As you probably know, many relationships like Lorraine's start in the rosy glow of hope, the honeymoon phase. But eventually you begin to show more of yourself to your partner. Hidden or unconscious parts of your personality come out.

Painful communication behaviors and problems start to cause stress and distance. Most of these conflicts come down to subtle or not-so-subtle examples of the attack-defend or pursue-withdraw pattern.

If you study the communications in these conflicts, you generally find that you and your partner strive to convince each other that "You are the problem." (It is so hard for most of us to admit that we are part of the problem! That admission would be too vulnerable, too scary.)

Arguments persist, because neither person wants to be blamed.

A key concept in couples' work is *self-responsibility*. It means turning the attention away from your partner, the apparent source of all bad things, and toward yourself.

When you become self-responsible, you are curious about your behavior. You begin to ask, "How am I creating this situation or this conflict?" Once you learn how to be curious about your reactions, you begin to understand an astonishing truth: **You are both equally responsible for the persistent repetition of conflicts**.

When you and your partner are on a path of healing and awareness, you feel that there is more love, compassion, energy, and vitality in your hearts. You want these feelings and energies to come out into your relationship, your family, and your community.

When you learn self-responsibility, you begin to speak to your partner in a more open and authentic way. You learn to create connections with your communication, and to take down the walls and defenses you have created.

Then you can deepen into an experience of love and awakening.

Let me continue with the client example above. The couple, Lorraine and Teddy, were in their late thirties. They had gotten married after eight years of living together in a committed relationship. Neither felt like their family respected their self-employed lifestyle choices or the partner whom they had selected.

Conflict in one session in my office centered on one of Teddy's cousins, who was dismissive of Lorraine at a holiday event. Lorraine was still infuriated two months later. When she spoke, I could see tense muscles in her neck. She sat up straight and stared across the couch at Teddy, "Who do you choose, your family or me? Why did you back your cousin instead of me? You do this all the time."

Teddy shrank a little and turned his head.

When I commented on his body movements, he said, "What am I supposed to do in the face of this onslaught? I have to be really careful. It usually gets worse."

Teddy will eventually understand how his caution may be part of the pattern of conflict with his wife, how his shrinking away infuriates her when she wants to be heard.

Lorraine started to cry, "This is so hopeless. How can I ever know what he is feeling when he is so careful all the time? How are we going to connect?" She wiped away a tear and looked down at the floor.

In this moment in my counseling office, Lorraine has revealed that she is longing for connection. She wants to know what Teddy is experiencing. She doesn't see how her anger makes it harder for her to get what she wants.

In this moment of potential opening, Teddy rose to the occasion beautifully. He came out of his shell and put his hand on hers. "I want that connection too, honey."

It's a great moment in counseling. The natural love and desire for healing in Teddy conquered his fear.

He said, in a voice soft but powerful, "I don't want you to feel despair when we get into this family feuding. It's my problem, I know."

"What do you want, Teddy?" Lorraine asked, still angry, but less so.

"I want you to know we can get through this. I can learn to listen better. My family is so repressed."

Lorraine's laugh suddenly brightened the room, "And you cannot stand them."

"True." He laughed as well. "It's you I love. I'm torn. I have to admit. I want to support you, and my family pulls on me to stay in their mess. When I try to make my own way, they hammer me."

Lorraine smiled again. "And then I hammer you as well. Maybe I'm just a little sensitive to being left out of the family group."

Lorraine continued, "We both feel like our families don't get us." Her face softened.

I relaxed as well, and Teddy leaned towards her again.

Authentic communication opens the doorway to hope, and to connection. When Lorraine touched her despair, and talked vulnerably about her pain, Teddy could feel it and could move toward her with empathy.

If on the other hand they stay in the attack-defense cycle, they will never create a feeling of safety. Anxiety will remain high and their communications will be defended.

But when Lorraine reveals herself, a vast space of love and consciousness opens up. Calmness and connection fill the room.

Lorraine and Teddy have begun to learn how to move from tension to intimacy. Using the Ten Practices, they can create and dwell in these moments of vulnerability and connection.

They can share the love that they both believe is possible.

Three Basic Skills: Self-Awareness, Self-Inquiry, and Self-Disclosure

Most couples, even those on a path of transformation, have not learned to practice communicating in an authentic, vulnerable way. This style of communication, the key to all the benefits which can come from the Ten Practices, requires three basic skills.

Couples who diligently work on these skills can learn them. Our brains and hearts are actually wired for connection and empathy! (See Rick Hanson's *Buddha's Brain*, New Harbinger Publications, 2009.)

Self-Awareness

Self-awareness is the first skill. It means awareness of the sensations that originate within your own body, such as your breathing, your posture, tight or stressed sensations in the body, your tone of voice, and body language.

Most of you don't pay attention to the internal world of your feelings. During your habitual conflicts, your body gives you many signals about anxiety, fear, or anger, but you were probably trained as a child to ignore them.

Self-awareness is a synonym for "mindfulness," a popular concept nowadays.

In relationships, self-awareness is the skill of being able to notice what happens right in that moment of stress or tension, the exact moment when the connection with your partner breaks down.

Many of my students have said, "So what? I can become aware of my body sensations. How does this mindfulness affect the conflict that we have?"

This is a great question.

You can transform your habits of communication if you start focusing not on what your partner did wrong but on what your actual experience is.

Take this client example: A couple in their early thirties, Jim and Karry, were in my office complaining of incessant power struggles. Today's dispute involved the scheduling of errands.

"You said you'd be back by twelve and it was almost one," she said.

Jim was shaking his head. "That's not what I said." Of course, he has his own story about the time agreement.

Karry continued, "When he looks like that and shakes his head, I know he thinks I'm an idiot. I get madder."

"Okay," I said, interrupting a familiar escalation. "Karry, you are guessing what he is thinking. It's true that you get madder. What does that feel like in your body? What starts to happen then?"

I wanted to show her how she tends to accuse Jim when she has a powerful internal experience, most likely fear or anger.

When Karry attacks Jim, he defends himself, a classic couples' interaction. This pattern causes each of them so much suffering and is one of the main reasons they are in counseling.

"I get hot and I want to point my finger at him and shake it."

"Good," I said. "What other feelings might be there?"

Karry got quiet. "I'm so mad." She took a deep breath and her neck relaxed. "Okay. Let me slow down. When he is gone and I don't know where he is, I get scared. I feel anxious."

"How do you experience that?"

"It's like a little quivering in my chest." Karry has begun to notice her own body signals and to report on them.

Then she continued, "I want to know where he is. " She teared up a little. "I need to know where he is."

Suddenly Jim turned his body a little towards her. As Karry softened, Jim started to respond empathetically to her.

Karry has begun to change her habit of blaming and mind-reading. But she cannot do this without practicing self-awareness.

Karry told us a month before in a session that her father and mother separated several times when she was about five or six. When her father left the house, she couldn't sleep, because she did not know where he was, or when he might come back.

Eventually Karry will see the connection between her childhood history and her anxious, angry attacks on her partner. (Certainly Jim has to be on time and be clear about his agreements.) But this story is important because it shows how becoming self-aware is a key factor in changing bad habits.

The story also shows how Jim's empathy can arise when Karry is aware of her inner hurts and experiences and begins to reveal herself. Then he can understand where the hurt comes from.

Here's the good news.

If you look at the range of emotions that children display, you can see that humans are naturally wired for complex emotional experience and sensation.

By using the Ten Practices, Karry, and you, can become much more aware of complex inner feelings.

This self-awareness is the first key skill that helps you to create new pathways in your brain, new pathways for consciousness, and for choice.

Self-awareness takes you deep into your own body, where all the positive feelings you want to experience–joy, bliss, intimacy, sexuality, peace, love, and kindness–are stored, inside our precious envelope of skin!

Self-Inquiry

Often when you are in a conflict, you play out a version of attacker-defender with your partner. One of you attacks (judges, criticizes, blames) and the other defends (withdraws, retreats, goes silent.)

A painful exchange like this can escalate, can go on for hours, and cannot lead to intimacy.

You just don't want to admit that you might have caused the conflict!

A vignette will dramatize this form of interaction. A mid-thirties couple came into my office a few years ago. Both had high-powered executive jobs. After some introductory history taking, I asked what patterns they would like to work on.

Lisa took the lead, "He is so secretive. He hides things from me. He doesn't tell me the truth about anything."

"Okay, I had a problem with drinking, but I stopped years ago," Terry said. "She is so invasive. Where did you go? Who were you seeing? I have no space to breathe. Of course I hide things."

Before Lisa could respond, I interrupted, to break the predictable exchange. I want her to practice self-awareness, then self-inquiry.

"Lisa, what are you actually feeling when you pursue Terry with questions?"

"He won't tell me anything, so probably some anxiety. My chest is tight. I keep reaching out to Terry, to make a contact, to get some reassurance."

Terry looked interested, "You want some reassurance? You just seem angry."

"Okay. What else do you think is there, near your chest?" I ask.

"Even when I get Terry's attention, I still want more of a sense of connection." Lisa was quiet a moment. "There is a feeling of urgency. I can feel it. Wow. I can see how he would want to push me away."

Terry relaxed and nodded.

"Yeah, like it's never enough, so I keep failing," Terry said. (He has revealed a lot about himself and his role in the pattern, but in this example, I'll concentrate on Lisa.)

"It never seems like enough. Like there is this hole in my heart."

"And what does that remind you of?"

"Nothing," Lisa said. "This tightness seems permanent. It's always been a part of me."

"What happens when you breathe into it?" I asked. "When you slow down and bring your attention to the tightness."

"Okay. Well it relaxes. And now I'm thinking about how my father left my mother. Weird, huh? I was away at summer camp, and when I came home, all his stuff was gone. He went to another state. I sat on the back porch all summer, imagining he'll come back. After that, my father came and went. But I never knew when I would see him."

"So maybe when you feel this strong need to stay in touch with Terry, it reminds you of your father, and missing him so much?" I asked gently.

"I never thought of it like that before. But the feeling is similar."

I'm condensing several sessions here, to show how self-inquiry changes bad habits of attack and defense. **Lisa began to see how her angry attacks covered up her feelings of needing the connection with Terry.** And as Lisa began to describe her desire for connection, Terry found the courage to move towards her, to reveal more of himself to her. (His strategy of protection had started with a critical father!)

Debra and I have struggled with this mode of attack-defend as well. As therapists, we joke that we are uniquely qualified to blame the other. For us, like many other couples, our early training didn't help us resolve conflicts.

We use many of the skills in the workbook, including self-disclosure and the time-out (Practice Six) to help us tune into ourselves, our bodies and our reactions, so that we can move toward understanding and connection.

Self-Disclosure

With this skill, you talk about the information you have discovered about yourself while practicing self-awareness and self-inquiry explorations with your partner.

Normally, your self-disclosure will help your partner understand why you might have reacted the way you did. Such understanding leads to the healing of those small breakdowns in trust and connection that occur in most relationships.

Lorraine and Teddy, a couple I described earlier, learned how their self-disclosure could help each other feel more empathy. This empathy soothes our fears and anxieties and allows for connection.

Here's another example:

Just last week, I was working with a couple, married for thirty-two years. Tomás had a continuing experience of being frustrated by his wife's lack of sharing her emotional life with him.

Angela had grown up being criticized for speaking up about her internal experience, feelings, and perceptions, so she was very careful.

Tomás said, "I've experienced her refusal to let me in so many times, and I feel frustrated. She never says anything."

Angela, who was in her early sixties, said, "Well, I feel his frustration, and I freeze. "

I asked Tomás, "What else do you experience in this pattern?"

"Well, I've been angry a hundred times. The more angry I get, the more she shuts down. So after the frustration, I feel lonely. Like we just cannot make contact."

I said, "Which do you think comes first, the anger or the loneliness?"

"I miss Angela a lot, so that's what probably comes first."

"Which do you talk about more?"

"The frustration." He was quiet a moment. "I see what you are getting at."

"When you feel lonely and then frustrated, you cannot make contact. Then what happens for you?"

Tomás's tone is quieter, more thoughtful. "I feel hopeless. I'll never get the love I need. "

Angela started leaning toward him, and she said, "I had no idea that you felt lonely." She reached out and touched his arm. There was more work ahead for this couple, practicing openness, but Tomás could begin to see how his vulnerability led to the connection he wanted.

Tomás can now understand how his anger pushes Angela away and perpetuates the pattern. When a person recognizes that their behavior is part of the pattern, they can begin to change their reactions.

Our unconscious reactions can lead to unwise and unkind speech, and perpetuate the patterns that cause pain. Tomás's vulnerability results in Angela moving towards him.

Examples of Self-Disclosure
It is not:
- Using broad generalizations: "You always... You never..."
- Blaming: "You were more unconscious than I was."
- Judging/Analyzing: "You are wrong. You are weak, immature, stupid, numb ..."
- Withdrawing: "I have nothing to say about that."
- Guessing/Intuiting: "When you get that look, I know what you are thinking."
- Confusing: "I feel that you always ..." (Usually a guess or a judgment follows.)
- Parsing through who said what at what time: "You got angrier when I told you the truth that you were always late. That's when you said..."
- Being right or making wrong: "I'm right about how the dishes go in the dishwasher. You don't know anything."
- Repeating stories about past injuries and mistakes.

Good self-disclosure contains one or more of these elements
- Physical sensations in the body: "I feel a fluttery feeling in my stomach." "My jaw is tight."
- Emotional descriptions, specific and in the moment: "I feel sad when I hear you talking about this."

- Self-Disclosure: "This feeling reminds me of my interactions with my father.
- Present time: "I feel like crying now."

You can make a profound turn when you start to use self-responsible language, a turn toward maturity, toward intimacy, and toward creativity.

The three basic skills, self-awareness, self-inquiry, and self-disclosure, are key to this powerful development.

The connection you can create is like food for the heart. You can get used to living without it, but the deprivation has consequences in your relationship and your family.

When you feel more love, you are more resilient when life throws the inevitable challenges your way.

Tension diminishes. Joy returns. Cooperation comes in the front door and makes a home with you.

Working with Intentions

Many couples that are on the path of healing are looking for a vision of their relationship. You and your partner can use the intentions here, to both create that vision, and to note when you are behaving in a way that is still on the path.

The intentions also help you create the safety needed for a deep connection.

None of us is perfect. We get tired, reactive, or overwhelmed. Then we react angrily or withdraw.

But through the use of intentions, you begin to believe that you and your partner will let go of protection, and find more empathy and understanding. It is easier for you to return to a feeling of intimacy and safety.

Many relationships start with vows and intentions, but then what happens? You are distracted by day-to-day responsibilities and commitments. You don't revisit your deepest aspirations on a regular basis. These aspirations, which form a powerful vision for your relationship, don't become a day-to-day conversation, or a standard of behavior.

In this phase, the honeymoon is over! This period is a predictable phase of a long-term relationship. Without attention, you can act out beliefs that are learned in childhood. These beliefs operate in our unconscious mind. They can inform the way we view the world and how we create relationships.   The conscious use of intentions, as shown in Practice Four, provides a powerful antidote to childhood beliefs such as:

- I'm not good enough to be loved.
- No one listens to me.
- I have to conceal my feelings, or I will be shamed or punished.
- I cannot be a success.

If you hold the inner deep belief that "No one loves me," you are apt to interpret the actions of your friends and family through that lens.

Fortunately, current brain research shows the amazing healing capacity of the human brain; this data show intentions can actually alter the structure of the brain itself. **New neural pathways can be created along which new information, beliefs, and motivations can travel.** (Again, see Rick Hanson's book, *Buddha's Brain*.)

Using Practices Four and Ten, which focus on intentions, you and your partner can help each other incorporate simple but profound beliefs like:

- I am loved.
- I can reveal myself to you and you will listen to me.
- We can share a joyous life together.
- I can be happy and successful.

This support for new beliefs is one of the great gifts you can offer your partner.

In the large workshops that I present with my wife Debra, we ask attendees to state out loud an intention, such as "I will be self-responsible." After the intentions Practice, students often report a tremendous range of inner experiences: fear, excitement, safety, or compassion. (The same responses happen in couples' sessions.)

These strong reactions demonstrate how intention can release energy and create a new opening for transformation.

The intentions listed below are key to reworking old beliefs that were embedded in our psyches when we were children.

Seven Key Intentions

1.   I'm willing to create a safe, loving relationship with you.

The longer I work with people, the more I see how important it is that you name this intention. People can easily forget how important that goal is. When you forget it, you cannot pursue it mindfully.

When we feel loved, we feel safe, so it is important as well to create feelings of safety with your partner. Most of the patterns of conflict I describe start with a small internal sensation of fear, or anxiety.

The key anxieties that fuel most conflicts have these questions at their root: "Am I loved and protected?" and "Is there room here for me to grow?"

A couple I worked with recently demonstrated these basic fears. Tommie's parents were always threatening divorce and running out of money, so he became hyper-responsible, and anxious about survival. Barry was raised by a single mother who kept him close to her and was very concerned for his safety. His main fear was about his ability to create his own identity, his own space to be himself.

With these forms of conditioning, you can see how a pursuer-withdrawer pattern could arise and cause lots of stress.

One antidote to this pattern is the first intention. When you say to your partner "I want a safe, loving relationship," you are also saying, "I want to create a relationship in which we can grow together, and in which we can feel loved and protected." What a powerful statement!

2.   I'm willing to notice what happens in my body when I start to feel anxious or distant.

As a child, you were probably taught to ignore the subtle signals your body was giving to you. Your parents or caregivers wanted you to behave, to conform to some mysterious social norm.

So you didn't learn to pay attention to the emotional and physical information your body was giving you all the time.

In relationships, if you don't notice these small moments of discord or tension, then you are vulnerable to being overwhelmed by stronger, negative feelings. That process is how the reactive patterns get stimulated.

By paying attention to the moment-by-moment experience of your body, you can heal small breaches of connection before they get magnified into conflict.

Self-awareness is inherently healing, because it means you are learning to look at yourself without judgment.

3. *I'm willing to study my predictable reactions to stress, so I can heal my unconscious responses.*

Few of us saw our parents or any adults studying their reactions in their relationships when we were younger, so how could we learn this skill?

It is an act of discipline, a practice, to turn your attention inward. You have to develop curiosity about your inner world. You have to open to deeper knowledge about yourself; yes, how you were hurt, but also how you can experience your deepest longings and passions.

Self-inquiry is a form of awareness, and awareness heals you, through a strange and mysterious process that allows you to love yourself more, and to make better choices about your behaviors and reactions.

Without self-study, you remain protected, locked in your safe known world.

When you express this intention, you open up to receive new emotional information about yourself.

4. *I'm willing to be self-responsible in my communications.*

As a child, when a conflict arose, you might have seen blaming and defending. Apologies may have been all too rare. So you learned to defend yourself, and to protect your ego, your position, or your opinion.

The fourth stated intention creates a high standard for communication.

Self-responsibility means being curious about your own inner world. Self-responsibility opens the door to your personal vulnerability, to your deep sharing about your experiences.

Self-responsibility is a widely used concept in couples work, and I have converted this important idea into three basic learnable skills: self-awareness, self-inquiry and self-disclosure.

Using these skills, you learn to understand yourself and to reveal more of your inner life to your partner. You learn to amplify the love and compassion you feel for your partner.

5. I'm willing to listen to you as deeply as I can.

When you were a child, your natural, authentic protestations and exclamations may have been ignored by adults who were not able to listen to you, for any number of reasons.

So you probably grew up not learning how to listen deeply and carefully to others, including your partner. While listening to a person talking, your attention may drift into your own reactions, or you may start planning the next thing you will say.

Deep listening means that you actually pay attention to your partner, that you be present when they are talking to you. You allow them the natural expression of their joy or sorrow.

With this intention of deep listening, you and your partner create a strong field of connection, in which love and honesty can flourish.

You hear about your partner's losses, hard feelings, and upsets, and you don't dismiss them. You pledge to listen, to stay in the relationship and to care.

Your presence and caring help your partner open to inner truths that they may have never known before. This opening leads to less self-judgment and better self-esteem. Your partner starts to think, "Well, if I have this thought or experience and my partner still loves me, I must be okay." This is a beautiful gift you can give to your partner.

This opening, to love, to ease, and to creativity, which you and your partner can create together, has no limits.

You can learn to experience more of these essential states with the discipline of deep listening.

6. I am willing to use time-out to stop our habituated conflicts.

You probably learned as a child that conflicts between adults lead to either escalation or to withdrawal. Some of these conflicts may have persisted for years, even decades, without any healing or letting go. The adults likely had no skills for conflict resolution or for insight into the causes of their behavior.

For example, my uncles warred with my father for years over decisions made in the family business. I didn't talk to my cousins for a long time, even though we went to the same high school. How painful!

You are learning the practices because you want to change painful patterns of conflict. Practice Six: Time-Out is an important tool to reach this goal.

Time-out is a conscious way of stopping the physical and emotional escalation. It is a middle road between attack and withdrawal. With the time-out, you and your partner agree to stop the escalation, so you can study your internal world.

All of us get flooded by internal sensations, and while flooded, we go directly into our patterns, without "passing Go and collecting $200."

Time-out leads to a new belief: Conflict can teach you about yourself, and lead to deeper connection with your partner.

7. I'm willing to use new communication skills to have a creative, happy life with you.

You probably learned how power struggles work. When two people disagree, someone wins (gets their way) and someone loses. So you think that the inevitable struggles between you and your partner over issues like money, time, and plans will create trouble.

What if this belief is wrong? Would it be okay for you if you lived in a state of continual happy collaboration? What beliefs or behaviors would you have to change?

With your partner, you will make hundreds, maybe thousands of decisions, in the course of your relationship. But how many of you will study how creativity and collaboration work?

Sadly, you can often find time for a five-hour or five-day power struggle, but you won't take a half an hour to do a practice that could heal these struggles forever!

Couples on the path of healing have the opportunity to experience the immense power of collaboration, to learn the beautiful creativity that is possible when people remain open and connected to each other while having differences of opinion.

The differences can become a form of creative friction, which forces you to dream up new, better solutions. Or these differences can drive you and your partner into emotional turmoil and distance. Which would you prefer?

As a child, you absorbed information from the people around you, and this information about relationship and communication became your own belief system and the underpinning of your communication habits.

Fortunately, consciousness and new intentions help these beliefs and behaviors to change.

Debra and I use Practice Four every week. For example, when we have a hot-button issue, like money or intimacy, we sit down and meditate for a few minutes (Practice One). Then, we state our intentions, and by doing so, honor the depth of the topic and how it could stir us to unconscious reactions.

We have learned that intentions are powerful tools for creating new, shared beliefs about better communication, about resolving power struggles, and about collaboration and creativity.

Couple's Creativity or Frequent Power Struggles? It's Your Choice

I sometimes say to my clients, "Think of all the time you spend on subtle conflicts over errands, responsibilities or agreements." Over the course of a long relationship, a couple must decide so many things together; some as simple as who takes out the garbage, and others like dealing with a sick child or a career change.

These decisions can be made from a feeling of love, harmony, and creativity, or they can be made as a series of repetitive, draining power struggles.

Through the Practices in the book, you can tap into a creative power that maximizes your good ideas and builds on the ideas and opinions of your partner.

This radical idea is based on the simple assumption that when you are connected to your partner, when you actually care about their ideas or their desires, you feel more creative. And so does your partner.

You can harness your creativity together, instead of blocking each other.

These power struggles are easy to describe. Instead of a creative, happy conversation about a project or plan, you feel anxious or tense. A power struggle is not necessarily loud and angry. It can be subtle, and still drain energy out of the relationship.

It's fine to disagree, to have different ideas about how things should happen. So why do you get stimulated into these predictable escalations of fear and anger?

I'll tell you. When you fear you won't get what you want, you can be triggered. The power struggles that you create are often arguments about who has the best idea or solution. These arguments tend to be about the content: the next action, plan or decision.

Often during the argument, a subtle fear is triggered, that you won't be heard, that you won't get what you need, or that no one is listening to you.

As with the communication conflicts described earlier in this book, unconsciously you project old injuries and reactions onto current situations with your partner. The emotions escalate intensely, and finally you ask yourself, "What was that all about?"

Fortunately you can bring more consciousness and better communication habits to these types of struggles. You can learn to:

- Be more creative, positive and loving.
- Work together more harmoniously and joyfully.
- Become more open to new ideas and suggestions.
- Be a better listener.

Power struggles share similarities to interlocking patterns of conflict in your relationship.

A client example might be useful here. I've been working with Bob and Jennie for a few months on the communication model, and they came in to one session laughing.

"Dodged a bullet," Bob said. "Almost had World War III."

"Bob started washing our new car," Jennie added. "Of course, he wasn't doing it right. "

"Actually," Bob interrupted, "She was putting the wrong soap on the bumper."

"Then he barked at me. I, of course, withdrew into my shell. I let him go a little longer washing the car with his soap while I was preparing my revenge. Then I told him that we didn't have enough time to finish it if he was going to take so long," Jennie laughed.

Bob laughed again, "Right about then we decided that we needed a time-out. While I was taking a walk around the block I asked myself, what was going on? Why was I so irritated? Then I realized that I was so stressed out about our company's future buyout, and also I had to work on my aunt's estate. I didn't think I had time to listen to Jennie's input."

"When he came back and talked to me about that," Jennie said, "I totally understood. And I could see how I had felt unheard, and pouted and got back at him. We decided to wash the car later."

"So if you think of this as a power struggle, what went wrong?" I asked.

"Everything," Bob said. "From the beginning it wasn't clear who was in charge, or how we were going to do the car washing."

"I got stimulated and started pushing my way," Jennie said. "I never asked Bob how he wanted to wash the car."

"I assumed that Jennie would do it exactly as I learned as a kid." Bob laughed and continued, "I never listened to Jennie's alternative ideas. When things went south, I blamed her."

"So I felt not heard," Jennie said, laughing again. "I can laugh now. It was a perfect storm of our defenses and habits. But it worked out well. Here we are."

Jennie and Bob are becoming aware of their power struggle habits and styles, and they are bringing more happiness and collaboration into their lives.

Bringing Consciousness to Power Struggles

Most power struggles have these basic components:

- You don't create clear agreements about how the project will be done or who's in charge before you start.
- Neither of you listens deeply to the other's needs and hopes.
- There is a lack of communication about the process; you each start with assumptions that turn out to be false.
- When one of you is stimulated into a reactive position, you push your position, or you withdraw. Each of these habituated responses leads to a negative outcome: resentment, misunderstanding, and frustration.

- Time is short, and you apparently need to rush. I ask my students though, "Why do you have an hour for a power struggle, but not ten minutes to get centered and exchange information?"

Predictable Patterns

As most couples know, these power struggles can persist for years, without some attempt to heal them.

By paying attention and by doing Practice Seven, you can experience more cooperation, generosity and joy. And more productivity.

Here are some common styles that people take on when they want to create something. If one partner consistently takes one of these roles, the other partner will probably also play a specific matching role. These roles can be the seedbed of great collaboration, or they can cause suffering and pain.

The Initiator: Initiators are great; they get things going. But they can also dismiss other's ideas. These types can say to their partner, "My way is better. Yours is more uninformed, stupid, tasteless..."

The Optimistic Idealist: These types say, "Oh, this will be so easy!" Their confidence and hopefulness can be great aids to creativity. They can be a little naïve! The Idealist can attract a Resistor, who brings the idea down to earth with a thud.

The Resistor: Resistors often want to gather a lot of information before going forward, and this is good. However, some people only feel powerful when they say No. They are too frightened to know what they want, or to say what they want. The research can be a way of delaying a decision.

A resistor has to be asked, "What do you want to do?" They have to get over their storehouse of objections by making a choice. (I used to be like this. Healing the pattern meant finding the courage to express myself.)

The Researcher: Getting all the data is important, for smart choices. But some people will delay decisions indefinitely, because they don't have enough information. They are afraid of conflict, or of upsetting their partner.

The Agreeable One: This type says yes. They can be very cooperative and helpful. But sometimes their "Yes" isn't fully thought out. Obstacles tend to arrive into the process almost accidentally.

The Depressed Type: These poor folks have lost the spark of creativity and hope, on a subtle level, so they get stuck in their current situation. Change is terrifying. They need to find a way to create more energy.

You may have a pattern that I haven't identified here. That's great, if you are able to identify it, investigate it, and heal it.

If you are creating power struggles, you can use the mindfulness and communication practices to become more aware of your reactions and to transform them.

Great creativity awaits you!

Creating Positive Conditions for Success and Collaboration

People tend to rush into decisions without sufficient communication. The bigger the decision, the more time should be devoted to it. Time is needed so that:

- Each of you says all your needs and hopes, without being dismissed or disregarded.
- Each of you describes your vision of how the project should go.
- Each of you is respected for your opinion and desires.
- You make an intention to use authentic communication to stay connected and open to each other.
- You agree on a solution to a problem or the next step in a project. Both of you feel good about the solution, even if it is a compromise. (This is key: a win-win.)

If either of you doesn't feel good about the solution, one of you has lost a power struggle. If this pattern happens frequently, resentment will build up.

When my students get to this stage of agreement, my office fills with stories of victories of consciousness over bad habits. Like with Bob and Jennie, I hear laughter and joy.

When you give up struggle, you have energy for joy and intimacy.

Chapter 3: The Ten Practices

Your long wait is over. Here are the Practices, beginning with some general notes and tips.

- The Practices are intended to develop skills in mindfulness and communication. These skills cannot be learned quickly! The Practices should be repeated several times.
- Some Practices call for you to do a visualization while your partner reads the instructions to you. Other Practices are intended to start an important mutual conversation, and are not divided up into Reader/Listener roles. This will be obvious when you read the Practice instructions.
- When you are the Reader, remember to read the directions slowly.
- Each practice begins with a brief description. Some conclude with ideas for further study or conversation.
- The practice directions assume that you are in a sitting position, facing your partner, to begin. The exercises start with both of you closing your eyes and taking a few deep breaths to connect with your body and with your partner.
- When the instructions call for the Listener to speak, the Reader should just listen, without interjecting any comments. This pure attention is a powerful gift to the speaker.
- Usually each of you will do the exercise, so set aside a specific amount of time for each of you. When I give a length of time for a Practice, that length is for one of you to go through the instructions. When you are finished with the Practice, you can switch roles then, or at a later time.
- Most Practices can be done in less than half an hour. You might need a timer for some Practices.
- Be sure to thank each other at the end of the Practice.

Practice One　　Being Present, or "Here I Am"

In our busy lives, we often fill our days with plans, errands, responsibilities, emails, and work tasks. But when we get caught up in life's minutiae, it's easy to forget some of the deeper possibilities of love and awareness.

Debra and I both use this simple Practice throughout the day when we are sitting with our students and clients, standing in line at the bank, washing dishes, or whatever. This Practice is inherently relaxing because you only have to think about one thing at a time.

Being present with your partner is a conscious act of love. You let go of other thoughts, breathe, and come into deep contact with yourself. **This is where intimacy begins, inside of your body.**

This Practice can help you transition from the everyday world of thinking and planning into the world of connection. Debra and I often follow these steps as we begin a creative conversation, or when we are sharing (self-disclosing) after a conflict or stressful conversation.

This Practice can take ten minutes or be extended for a half an hour.

Steps
1.　Reader: "Close your eyes and take a few breaths into your body. Feel the weight of your body in your chair. Feel how your breath moves through the body, the actual subtle movement of your lungs, your stomach or your shoulders."
2.　Reader: "Keep your attention focused on your breath. Note if there are any distracting thoughts and just let go of them. Return your attention to your breath."
3.　Reader: "Notice any tense muscles in your body, in your face, shoulder, or in your stomach, for example. Try to relax the tension, using small movements of those muscles or by breathing into the tight places."
4.　Reader: "Now focus on your breath, and we will be quiet together for three to five minutes."
5.　After this time elapses, Reader: "Now bring into your mind for a few moments some simple intention for our relationship, such as the intention to connect, to be open, to tell the truth. Let yourself feel the emotional impact of meditating on that intention."

6.   Reader (Softly): "Now take a few breaths and when you are ready, you can open your eyes and we can talk about the Practice."
7.   Reader and Listener can discuss their experiences of being quiet together, or the Listener can talk about the impact of meditating on the intention.
8.   Remember to thank each other!

Notes

After a few experiences of this Practice, you will not need the instructions when you do it.

Appendix 2 gives you more complete meditation instructions. I recommend to most of my students that they have a regular practice, like meditation, yoga, chi gong, tai chi, or something else that reminds them of the invisible world, the Great Mystery, the interconnection of all beings, or whatever you call it.

A Path for Couples points you towards this mysterious world! Our culture keeps our thoughts and attention mired in the economic and psychological parts of our psyche. This habituated thinking does not cultivate our relationships.

Practice Two   Appreciation–What Your Partner Deserves!

When we appreciate our partner, in their beauty, responsibility, thoughtfulness, or other attributes, we give them a powerful gift. The gift of love. It opens the heart of the listener and the speaker. This sense of connection is healing. It soothes us and lowers our anxiety. We feel happy!

Strangely, most of us need practice to cultivate these powerful, connected states with our partners. During a simple appreciation Practice in my office, Thomas, one of the partners, made a strange gulping sound.

When I asked him about it, he said, "I felt something powerful in my heart, and the sound just flew out of me. I thought my partner knew how loyal I was to him, but when he said it, I felt truly known by him. My heart just burst open." He wiped a tear from his eye and continued, "I am loyal, and I love this man so much."

Now his partner leaned close to him and said, "I know you so deeply, and I love you."

Rarely will we reveal ourselves so deeply to the ones we love without coaching or without specific practices. And our partners have seen us at both our most powerful moments and our weak or troubled ones, and they still love us. How cool is that?

Practice Two asks you to spend five minutes praising your partner. And you can do this Practice once a day (or whenever you like).

Steps
1.   Reader: "Please close your eyes. Then take a few breaths with me. Now imagine a few things that you appreciate about me. Start with the practical world that we share. What do you appreciate about the way I take care of you, of our family? What do you appreciate about the things I do? Earning a living? Rearing children? Volunteering? Taking care of our house? Wanting a healing relationship?"
2.   Reader: "Now think about my inner qualities, the qualities of my inner or essential self. (Examples: courage, generosity, kindness, and forgiveness of others.) What inner qualities do I have that you appreciate?"

3.   Reader: "Now open your eyes, and we can discuss what you appreciate about me." The Listener shares for a few minutes, till he or she is done.

4.   Reader: "Now we can discuss the feelings that arise in both of us when listening or speaking these appreciations." Five or ten minutes.

5.   Remember to thank each other.

Note

If you feel really courageous, you could try this practice every day, in a less formal way. Sneak up on your partner while they are doing the dishes and praise them!

Practice Three   Communication Model 1–Can We Talk?

In this practice, you study a recent repetitive conflict or stressor. This would often be an attack-defend or a pursue-withdraw pattern, as I discussed in Chapter 2. Our unconscious is highly creative and invents many variations on these basic themes!

For the first use of the model, as Practice Three, do NOT use a pattern you get into with your partner. We want to build up a whole series of skills first.

Instead, think of a recurring specific reaction you have to various situations. It could be that you feel defensive, attacked, judgmental, or critical. For example, some people feel very defensive and they withdraw when they are given feedback.

You are looking for a reaction that you have in a variety of situations with different people. This repetition is important information for you, because it usually points to some of your earlier conditioning or training.

When you use Practice Three, you become more mindful of your habits and patterns. You "become friends" with your actual experience.

I recommend that you do this Practice several times, studying and writing down the reaction you have each time. As time goes by, you will experience more versions of the same pattern.

Using the form in the appendix, you will write down more and more information about this specific pattern of reactions. Over time you will become more aware of your actual sensations. (Self-awareness) You will understand how you might have learned your reaction. (Self-inquiry) And you will learn to talk about this pattern in a new way. (Self-disclosure) Then you will be able to make better choices about your behavior.

As you work on these basic communication skills, they become easier. As you build up the skills, the Practice will direct you to patterns with your partner. (These patterns are more challenging to work with!)

This Practice takes twenty to thirty minutes.

Steps

1.   You discuss with your partner a specific reaction you have when confronted with stress or disagreement. Try in a few minutes to

identify such a pattern, using the examples above. Listen carefully to feedback from your partner, who is here to help you with this inquiry. Then take these steps.

2.   Reader: "Let's take a few deep breaths together now."

3.   Reader: "Please close your eyes. Imagine the last time you were in the pattern. Where were you? What do you remember about the surroundings? Were you are work or with a friend or family member? Were you indoors or outdoors? What was the topic you were discussing? When did the tension or stress begin to arise in your body?"

4.   Reader: "Now, turn your attention more deeply inward, towards yourself, and remember as deeply as you can everything you notice about the following, as I read to you. (Note to Reader: Read slowly and pause after reading each question.)

• What was the first physical or emotional signal that you were beginning to feel stressed, distant or upset? Did you go into a predicable pattern then?

• Did you begin to feel anxious, angry or separate then?

• What is the first thing you remember saying?

• What was your tone of voice? Did you notice any changes in the way you were talking? (Louder, slower, quieter, more urgently?)

• How did your breathing change when you went into your response?

• What were your posture and body language? What were they expressing? What were they concealing?

• Did you have tight or stressed body tensions? Where in your body did you feel these?

• Did you notice any other body signals?

• What was the most predominant feeling you had? (Examples: anger, sadness, or loneliness.)

• Were there any more subtle feelings that might have been hard to notice?

• How does this pattern of feelings and reactions that you just described to me seem familiar from other relationships? From seeing one of your parents or siblings act this way.

• Have you had similar reactions before?

- What can you learn about yourself from studying these reactions? Your history of relationship? Your parents' influence
on you?

Please think about these questions for a few minutes. When you
are ready, open your eyes and you can take some notes."

5.   Reader: "Now using the simple form from Appendix 3, write
down the answers to as many of the questions as you can. (Five minutes or more.)

6.   When the Listener is done, Reader: "Will you read your notes
to me now?" Listener reads.

7.   When the Listener is done reading, you can sit together quietly
for a few minutes. You may want to discuss the Listener's sharing,
now or at a later time.

8.   Then thank each other for your efforts to be conscious together.
A polite bow or hug is appropriate.

Notes

The skills of self-awareness, self-inquiry and self-disclosure
are interwoven with each other. Sometimes as you are disclosing,
more feelings arise, or another insight. Good for you!

After the Listener has shared, he or she can be quite tender or
quiet. This is not a good time for the Reader to make comments or to
bring up painful memories!

Over time as you do this Practice a few times, and fill in the form
with more details, you will probably realize that your unconscious
reactions to this type of situation didn't begin recently. You will understand more deeply how you were trained.

This information can help you understand some of the reactions you have in your relationship, which we will study later. And it
helps your partner not take your reactions so personally.

The Practices in the workbook seem simple. But they work to
substitute new habits for old ways of thinking and acting. So repetition is the key. You and your partner should do each of the Practices
several times. Change comes with discipline.

Practice Four   Working With Intentions–Creating a Vision

When you work with intentions, you are trying to change deeply held beliefs stored in your mind and body. (Research shows that the brain actually functions throughout the body, not just in the head.)

This is why the steps for this Practice ask you to do more than just think about the intentions or to simply say them.

Remember, you can use any of the seven intentions from Chapter 2 for this Practice. I would suggest taking one intention and focusing on it for a month. Do Practice Four with that one intention once a week. Then go on to the next intention the next month.

Try to feel these powerful intention statements deeply in your body, as you say them or hear them. Your body contains all your habits and patterns in the form of patterns of energy and information. These patterns lead to our relationship habits and reactions.

So the whole body is the place where change can occur. This Practice can be done in fifteen minutes.

Steps

1.   Reader: "Please close your eyes and take a few breaths. I'll read Intention One out loud to you now. 'I'm willing to create a safe, loving relationship with you.' I'll read the intention to you a few times. Please notice any physical or emotional changes in your body when I read it."

2.   Reader reads the intention a few times, and the Listener listens and follows directions.

3.   Reader: "Now, in your own words, say that intention internally a few times. Not out loud. You can change the words till they work for you. Again, note any changes in emotion, and any images or memories that occur while you repeat the intention to yourself."

4.   Reader: "Now, open your eyes, and looking at me, say the intention to me out loud a few times."

5.   Listener says the chosen intention out loud a few times.

6.   Reader: "Now, close your eyes. Again, do you notice any physical or emotional changes? Any images? Any memories?"

7.   After a few minutes, Reader: "Now, please open your eyes and let's talk about whatever you experienced as you were listening to the

intention, or saying it out loud." (Reader: you can say the following sentence as needed, "We are looking for self-disclosing language here, not a description of my flaws!") A revealing conversation ensues.
8.   Remember to thank each other at the end of the Practice!

Notes

All the intentions taken together help you create a powerful, conscious relationship, in which you will experience more joy, love and happiness. It's the repetition of the intention over months or years that has the biggest impact.

Remember, you are trying to change beliefs and habits that are in some cases decades old.

Practice Five   Communication Model 2 - I Didn't Know You Felt That

Many of the previous Practices build skills that will help you with Practice Five, in which you explore patterns that you have with your partner. The steps are similar to Practice Three in which you explored habituated reactions to specific situations with other people.

Of course, you may have noticed that emotional explorations are a little more intense with your partner!

You will work with your partner to identify a recent repetitive conflict that you have together. This would be an attack-defend or a pursue-withdraw pattern, as we discussed in Chapter 2. (See page 7 for a definition of these interactions.)

In our patterns and defensive postures, we are not mindful, and we are not revealing our inner world to our partner. As you do this Practice, using the form from Appendix 3, you write down more and more information about the specific pattern you've chosen. You become more aware of your actual sensations and reactions.

You learn to talk about these patterns as they arise. **Then you are able to make better choices about your behavior and to find your way back to a connection with your partner.**

This Practice can be done in twenty to thirty minutes.

Steps

1.   You and your partner discuss one of the patterns that you both agree is causing stress in your relationship. Try in a few minutes to identify a pattern without getting triggered in the discussion. Then take the following steps.

2.   Reader: "Let's take a few deep breaths together now."

3.   Reader: "Please close your eyes. Imagine the last time you were in the pattern. Where were you? What do you remember about the surroundings? Were you at work or with a friend or family member? Were you indoors or outdoors? What was the topic you were discussing? When did the tension or stress begin to arise in your body?"

4.   Reader: "Now, turn your attention more deeply inward, toward yourself, and remember as deeply as you can everything you notice about the following, as I read to you. (Note to Reader: Read slowly and pause after reading each question.)

- What was the first physical or emotional signal that you were beginning to feel stressed, distant or upset? Did you go into a predicable pattern then?
- Did you begin to feel anxious, angry or separate then?
- What is the first thing you remember saying?
- What was your tone of voice? Did you notice any changes in the way you were talking? (Louder, slower, quieter, more urgently?)
- How did your breathing change when you went into your response?
- What were your posture and body language? What were they expressing? What were they concealing?
- Did you have tight or stressed body tensions? Where in your body did you feel these?
- Did you notice any other body signals?
- What was the most predominant feeling you had? (Examples: anger, sadness, or loneliness.)
- Were there any more subtle feelings that might have been hard to notice?
- How does this pattern of feelings and reactions that you just described to me seem familiar from other relationships? From seeing one of your parents or siblings act this way.
- Have you had similar reactions before?
- What can you learn about yourself from studying these reactions? Your history of relationship? Your parents' influence on you?

Please think about these questions for a few minutes. When you are ready, open your eyes and you can take some notes."

5.   Reader: "Now using the simple form from Appendix 3, write down the answers to as many of the questions as you can. (Five minutes or more.)

6.   When the Listener is done, Reader: "Will you read your notes to me now?" Listener reads.

7.   When the Listener is done reading, you can sit together quietly for a few minutes. You may want to discuss the Listener's sharing, now or at a later time.

8.   Then thank each other for your efforts to be conscious together. A polite bow or hug is appropriate.

Notes

As you repeat this practice, and fill in the form with more information, you will probably realize that your unconscious reactions to your partner probably didn't begin in this relationship.

The Practices in this book seem simple. But they work to substitute new habits for old ways of thinking and acting. So repetition is the key. You should do each of the Practices in the workbook several times. Change comes with discipline.

Remember: When the Listener is reporting on the answers to the questions, the other keeps quiet and watches his or her own reactions.

If tension or conflict arises, use Practice Six, the Time-Out.

When your partner reveals vulnerable experiences and feelings to you, it is important to honor these revelations. He or she will be quite tender and open at the end of this practice.

Also, repetition is the key to authentic communication. As you tell your inner story over and over, many things happen:

- You become more familiar with your inner experience
- You learn how to talk about it in a vulnerable way.
- Your partner learns to feel compassion for your inner hurt or tension that causes the repetitive conflict.

Practice Six   Time-Out–Stop In the Name of Love and Return to Connection

The time-out is a procedure for de-escalating painful patterns with your partner. When you ask for a time-out, you acknowledge that you are having a bad reaction to a stressor, and that your biology (fight, freeze or flight) overwhelms you.

In my own mind, just before I call a time-out, I say to myself, "The next thing I am about to say is really stupid and reactive!" I know that if I keep talking when stressed or angry, more distance will arise between Debra and me, and it will be harder to repair. **This moment of mindfulness is critical to healing and growth.**

You can learn to calm yourself, and these tense situations with your partner will not be as painful or endure for as long.

There are two stages in creating a clear time-out. The first one occurs **before** you are triggered.

Before You Need the Time-Out

Steps
1.   Have a short discussion with your partner about why you want to use the time-out, and how it might work.
2.   You both agree on a simple signal that the time-out has begun: a verbal sign or a hand motion. (The signal doesn't mean anyone is wrong. It simply means that you have become aware of being flooded by overwhelming emotions.)
3.   You agree on the length of time that the time-out will last: five minutes, half an hour, perhaps an hour; and you also schedule the time you and your partner expect to continue the conversation. (Of course, this agreement can be tricky given busy work and parenting schedules!)

When You Need the Time-Out

Steps
1.   You notice that a conflict has begun. You feel tense, or maybe some distance has arisen between you and your beloved. (Self-awareness.)
2.   You realize that you may be too emotional or over-stimulated to use the communication model. (You are tempted to attack, defend, withdraw, or pursue.)

3.   You call a time-out, using the signal already agreed upon.

4.   You each take responsibility for your own reaction. The best way to do this is to use Practice Five. (Soon you will be able to do the practice without reading the steps.)

5.   After the agreed-upon time interval, each of you discloses what you have learned about yourself and what you have learned about the habit or stressful pattern that has arisen. Each of you takes five to ten minutes to express yourself while the other pays attention without interrupting.

(If tensions arise again after reconvening, it's fine to take another time-out.)

6.   Don't forget to say thank you and bow, even if you think the issue is unresolved.

Notes

You want to have the time-out procedure in place before you need it. Otherwise you may continue your fight with a new topic: How best to do the time-out!

Stopping a conflict that you have had many times is always a work in progress. Over time you will notice that revealing your deep emotional truth and expressing your needs is the best way to resolve a conflict and to return to connection. **(Seriously, you've tried blaming, defending, and withdrawing. How are these methods working for you?)**

Once you feel connected to each other, it is much easier to solve whatever problem has caused the stress. Sometimes after the time-out, one of the partners is still feeling vulnerable or reactive. If so, it's better to take another time-out than to return to an escalating conflict.

Soon you will realize that there is a path back to your partner when familiar stress creates distance. **That path is using the authentic communication model, intentions, and time-outs.** Using these Practices, conflicts become less amplified or dangerous.

One of the intentions in Practice Four specifically addresses being willing to use the time-out. If you do Practice Four, you will have another chance to talk about the time-out with your partner.

You can use the time-out during a Practice, or when you start to feel tense or distant from your partner.

Using the Practices helps us to be more conscious. Something in us wants to be vulnerable, and to change these patterns.

But sometimes time-out is the only way we can move towards the self-responsible language of disclosure, the magic balm that can heal distance.

Practice Seven   Creativity, Collaboration and Joy

If you are engaged in a creative project with your partner and you feel tense or separate, a power struggle is either already happening, or about to happen. Mindfulness can help you note when subtle tension begins to arise.

By power struggle, I don't necessarily mean a loud argument, but simply a failure to work happily and creatively together, a missed opportunity for connection and productivity.

In the three parts of Practice Seven, you can study how these subtle or intense struggles occur. You can learn to study your own psychology, so you can understand better what creativity patterns you have, and how they can be improved. Then you can experience more success, abundance and joy.

You can take note of how successful collaborations occur, so you can replicate them in the future.

Seven A - Collaboration and Joy
Steps
1.   Remember a successful project you did together. Discuss the following topics for five or ten minutes.

What were the shared feelings of success?

What were the conditions that allowed the project to be successful?

2.   Review material in Chapter 2 on Creating Positive Conditions for Success and Collaboration. Discuss how many of the conditions you achieved in your example project.

3.   Thank your partner!

Seven B - Moving from Power Struggle to Greater Creativity
Steps
1.   Discuss common issues and patterns that arise when power struggles occur. What role or position does each of you tend to take when initiating and discussing a project? (Look for patterns I described in Chapter 2. Take a time-out if tension arises during this discussion.

2.   Then take five-ten minutes each to work through Practice Five. Use the tools you have learned to discover more about your creativity style and challenges, and about what kind of communications you tend to exchange, in power struggles.

3.   Do Practice Four, using the intention: "I'm willing to have a creative, happy life with you."
4.   Create your own intentions, to move towards greater collaboration.
5.   Remember to thank your partner!

Notes

In these discussions, use the time-out and the communication model as needed.

By exploring the struggles that you co-create, you can become more aware of them. This awareness helps you to stay connected while you work with your partner. The connection is the main thing you need to preserve, so that you can make decisions more happily and creatively.

Seven C - More Collaboration and Happiness: The Advanced Course

Steps

1.   Identify a simple project that is coming up for a decision. Use Practice One, Being Present, to begin this conversation.
2.   Schedule sufficient time to discuss it in detail, at least a half an hour.
3.   Start with a simple version of Practice Four, using Intention 4. Say it to your partner. "I'm willing to be self-responsible in my commnication with you." Then your partner says the intention to you.
4.   Then pick the Reader and the Listener.
5.   Reader: "Please take five or ten minutes to speak freely and uninterruptedly about your ideas for the project's next step: your hopes, fear, excitement, solutions, and creative ideas." The Reader listens respectfully, without dismissing ideas or feelings.
6.   Switch roles and repeat Step 5.
7.   Work together to find the next step in a project. It is important that you find a next step that both you and your partner can agree to.
8.   Sit together for a few minutes quietly and breathe together.
9.   Then discuss how the process went. Did any patterns of struggle arise? What can you learn about yourself? Celebrate small victories of consciousness. You can always use time-out if tension arises.

Notes

Any pattern of creativity that you discover in yourself can be investigated, simply by asking, "How might I have learned this?" When you bring awareness to these patterns, you feel and act more happily and more consciously, particularly as you work with your partner.

If you start to feel disconnected during a conversation about a plan, you have created a struggle. Often, as a result, key information, either factual or emotional, is lost.

But it can come back and can drag down the creativity and positive feeling that you are trying to achieve. And it can affect the success of the project itself.

During a creative process, you want to stay connected to your partner. Happiness comes from making creative decisions together.

Note the tendency to hurry to a result. Clarity and listening can take some time at the beginning, but they save time later.

Practice Eight   Awareness of the Field–Is That You Over There?

Your body has an incredible system for picking up signals from your partner. Practice Eight creates more mindfulness, so you can read and understand these subtle messages.

You will also learn to take note of the "field" between the two of you.

The field is a subtle invisible web of connections. One way to understand it is to ask yourself the question: "How do I feel about my partner right now? Warm, neutral, numb, excited, connected?"

The field is like the atmosphere, or the weather between the two of you. It goes through many changes throughout the day, as you talk, go to work, make love, or argue. It is a dynamic, ever-changing sense of connection, neutrality or distance.

No judgment! The field evolves all the time. Sensing your connection with your partner is a key to the communication model described here.

If you start to notice tiny feelings of distance or isolation, you can learn to comment on them, using more vulnerable statements. Then your interlocking struggles will diminish in intensity, and you will experience more love and connection.

This Practice can be done in less than fifteen minutes.

May the Field be with you.

Steps
1.   Reader: "Think of all we have been through together, and for a moment, feel some gratitude for our shared journey. Notice how the field changes when you experience gratitude."
2.   Reader. "Imagine our relationship right now. How does it feel to you? Do you feel connected to me? Neutral? Distant? What does your body sense when I am near you now–when you are listening to me? Don't make any verbal responses until you are asked to."
3.   After a short pause, the Reader continues slowly: "Use a few words internally (not out loud) to describe that connection. Examples: Cool, close, far, loving, anxious, excited, warm, open, angry. Just take a few breaths and relax into the feeling. Try to name it. Explore the sensations of our connection, with no blame or judgment for either of us. Don't try to explain or tell a story, just note the

sensations. Try to use language that describes only your physical and emotional experience."

4.   Reader: "Now imagine if you could change the field between us, by making it a little warmer, a little more energetic. Maybe you would imagine a look, a touch, a statement of gratitude, or a word of praise." (Slight pause.)

5.   Reader: "Now imagine making that gesture, or saying that word, to me. How does your body respond? Do your emotions change? Does the field change?"

6.   Reader: "Please open your eyes now, and make that gesture or say those words to me." (Reader: Put the book down and be ready to listen! It only takes a few minutes for the listener to respond verbally.)

7.   Reader: "Let's talk to each other freely for a few minutes, without instruction or role: How did the exercise feel? Were you able to sense the field? To affect it? Was it hard? Easy?"

8.   Then the Reader can respond to questions that the Listener asks, such as "Was it easy for you to feel the warmth? What did you notice as you were receiving?"

9.   Remember to thank your partner for the exploration of consciousness.

Notes

When you first start using this Practice, it is best to do so when you feel connected to your partner, not when you feel upset or angry!

Often the field between the two of you changes during the exercise. After some practice sessions, the Listener can begin to comment on this. ("As I speak to you, I notice my heart warming up. I feel more open, more vulnerable.")

Noticing and commenting on these subtle emotional changes as they are happening is a key skill in developing authentic communication.

It may take a few repetitions of this Practice before you start to sense it.

**Practice Nine   A Positive Connection–Creating More Love
and Happiness**

The simple Practices here don't take a lot of instruction. But each one, done on a regular basis, will help you feel more connected and alive. Couples naturally want to feel good together, but sometimes as we rush around from task to task, we forget the simple ways we can make each other happy.

When we feel disconnected, tensions can easily arise. When we feel positive and connected, it is easier to enjoy life together.

Scheduling

Take your personal calendar and that of your partner and schedule one half to one hour a week to connect for the next month. Here are some suggestions: (No texting or multi-tasking permitted!)

- Take a walk; hold hands and enjoy the quiet together.
- Go bowling! (Some couples experience an absence of fun!)
- Follow the meditation instructions in Practice One. Or, sit quietly together holding hands. Follow your partner's breathing and breathe together in sync for five minutes.
- Or, you can watch television together. (Just kidding!)

Self-Care and Self-Care with Your Partner

When you or your partner is running on empty, it's so easy to be reactive. We have so many ways to recharge our batteries: a hobby, exercise, reading, gardening, walking, to name a few. These simple practices tend to be overlooked when we feel late or overworked.

So for the sake of the relationship, it is good to take care of yourself. The walk or the workout can include your partner! Having fun is not a waste of time. It is a vital way of nurturing your relationship and restoring physical and mental health.

Study and Learn Together

Read through the book together for at least a half an hour each week. Reading together gives you a common vocabulary for authentic conversations. It helps you see how couples can talk to each other, how intentions can become embedded in your daily life, and how to practice creativity and collaboration together.

You can find other books on relationship, meditation, or healing, as well. I won't be upset!

Gratitude: It's Good for Your Health!

Spend five minutes per day expressing gratitude to your partner (or five times a week if you don't have five minutes a day!) You can talk about both your relationship and its different positive qualities, and about life in all its incredible manifestations.

Steps

1.   Reader: "Please close your eyes. Take a few breaths with me. Imagine a few things that you feel grateful for. (Possible examples: for your health, for breathing, for our beautiful planet, and for friends and family. For being a couple with a path of love and transformation!)

2.   Reader: "Then imagine the practical world that we share. What do you feel grateful for in our life together? Our house, our family? Are you grateful for the things I do? Earning a living? Rearing children? Taking care of our house? Wanting a healing relationship?"

3.   Reader: "Now think about my inner qualities, the qualities of my inner self or my essential self. (Courage? Generosity? Kindness? Forgiveness for others?) What inner qualities do I have that you feel grateful for?"

4.   Reader: "What are you grateful for, in our relationship?"

5.   Reader: "Now you can open your eyes and we can discuss what you see in me and what you felt for a few minutes."

6.   An advanced practice/discussion for both of you: While you are discussing the gratitude that each of you has, notice and describe the positive feelings that come up.

7.   Remember to thank each other.

Practice Ten   More Key Intentions

As you know by now, you can learn how to exchange more positive energy with your partner. Working with intentions that focus on connection, love and creativity is a powerful method to accomplish this goal.

Examples of key intentions are:

- I'm willing to take care of myself so I can be more present with you.
- I'm willing to create more positive energy with you.
- I'm willing to learn better communication skills for creativity and for collaboration with you.
- I'm willing to have more fun with you.

You can benefit tremendously from using creative arts to integrate these intentions into your relationship. In creative arts, you use your whole body to receive and utilize new concepts and beliefs in a holistic, complete way. Brain research shows that when we use art, we can create new pathways for information and sensory input to travel along, and that these pathways can lead to new beliefs and behaviors.

Being mindful of pleasurable experiences and being with them deeply also retrains the brain and makes it able to have more positive experiences.

I'd recommend at least half an hour of creative arts activity for each intention that you create. You can use one or more of the art forms below.

- Writing: Write poetry or songs about each intention and recite or sing them to each other. Don't confine yourself to the short list above. Make up intentions that specifically address your own vision, needs and issues.
- Dancing: Make up a dance together that expresses one of the intentions. Do it together and laugh a lot. Pick out music that you both love for the dance.
- Drawing: Get out some large sheets of paper, crayons or paints and create a big picture together of how you would look as a couple if you were living in a state of positive energy. Talk

about how you will foster such positive feelings in each other. Make a collage of pictures and advertisements, and then add words and pictures.

- Make up your own art forms and instructions. Have fun. Giggle.

Steps

1.   Discuss the simple instructions above together, and decide on one art form to use, and one intention.

2.   Get out your schedules and book at least a half an hour.

3.   Party on! Feel those good feelings of being creative together!

4.   Discuss the good feelings that come from creating and visioning together.

5.   Thank each other.

Chapter 4: A Blessing for the Couple on the Path

Over the years, I have seen so many courageous couples use the Ten Practices for healing and for growth. These couples were dedicated to transforming their relationship into a path of awakening.

Using the Ten Practices regularly, you can expect the same results. You will feel more intimate with your partner, you will have better sexual connections (at any age), and you will learn to speak more honestly and authentically.

In the new trust that you create, you cease to protect yourself from your partner. You open up new powerful channels of communication, and you learn to share those private places of hurt or shame that you have never told anyone about.

In a class recently, a student said, "When I take responsibility and acknowledge my defensiveness and where it comes from, my partner is grateful. I feel this blessing coming from him. He can tolerate my humanness. I feel loved in a deeper way, a way that is healing, that helps me let go of the behaviors that hurt him. Tony really loves me, and loves and tolerates parts of myself I never could show to anyone before."

This is the true gift of a conscious relationship. It is the gift that Debra has given to me over the years.

The love and vitality that couples on the path of healing can create has a tremendous impact on their children, friends, relatives, and colleagues.

Each of the vignettes in this book shows how couples create painful recurring patterns. The stories also show how these habits and patterns can begin to change, when you bring loving attention and curiosity to these patterns.

When I think about the values of our Western culture, I see the big billboards on Lombard Street as I drive to my office in San Francisco. "Buy this." "You need this now." "What happens in Vegas stays in Vegas." All messages about desire and acquisition.

The billboards don't read, "Wake up now." "Be Kind." "Consciousness heals." We live in a sea of confusion and desire.

Thankfully, most of you are already aware of your need for discipline and for the Practices, if you want lasting change.

I offer you this blessing: May you have the courage, the discipline and the time to transform your relationship into a vehicle for love, joy, and awareness. And may the healing move out from you and your partner to your family, neighborhood and world.

APPENDIX 1
QUICK RELATIONSHIP COURSE FOR THOSE SHORT ON TIME

Most couples are short of time, of course!

You can experience more joy and less conflict in your relationship simply by doing the following things well:

1. *Notice painful repetitive patterns as they arise.* Without moments of awareness, couples can create the same patterns over and over, for years. With awareness, we have the chance to be less reactive, and to make better choices.

2. *Practice authentic, vulnerable self-disclosure.* Often when we are reactive, we talk about our partner, what they could have done, or what they should have done, or what they really meant. We need to learn how to talk about ourselves in an open way. Use the communication techniques described in Chapter 2.

3. *Be curious.* Talk about your relationship connections and disconnections with your partner, for at least thirty minutes a week. (Sorry, not while answering email and watching TV.) Discuss vignettes and insights into your own patterns of communication and behavior.

4. *Practice taking a time-out when you get overwhelmed by negative emotions.* We all get carried away by strong reactions in stressful situations. As children we learned, "Take a deep breath." This is still great advice.

5. *Notice the times when you and your partner feel a strong positive connection.* Commit yourself to learning how to create those moments. Couples have to build time commitments into their lives that support happiness and connection.

6. *Notice the first breakdown in the subtle connection between you and your partner and be willing to talk about it in the first moment you feel it, without blame or judgment.* These small moments of separation create distance, and the distance can build up until you find yourself in an argument.

7. *Create intentions together with your partner.* Many people state powerful intentions when they make a commitment to each other (such as an engagement or marriage), then they never really think about them again. Key Intention: "I'm willing to be curious and vulnerable in my communications with you." Focus on this intention for a week.

8. *Listen, listen, listen.* When we get reactive, we stop listening. Then our partner doesn't feel heard. This dismissal and rejection pattern usually recreates a trauma from childhood when no one was listening to us. Be willing to observe your own reactions, and just listen. Many disagreements will fade away when you practice this simple skill.

APPENDIX 2
BODY-AWARENESS MEDITATION INSTRUCTIONS

There is a reason why meditation or contemplation has been practiced by spiritual seekers for at least three thousand years. **It calms the mind, opens the heart, and allows the meditator access to experiences of compassion and awareness that are otherwise unavailable in 'normal' consciousness.**

You can read these steps to your partner, or read them to yourself. After several meditations, you will not need to read. Meditating together is a powerful way to connect.

1. Reader: "Sit down, with your back straight in a comfortable position. Feel your weight on the chair or seat. Bring your attention inside your body. Let go of any thoughts of planning or of responsibilities that are attracting your attention. Let go of the future and the past."

2. Reader: "Bring your attention, the focus of your concentration, to the here and now, on the sensations inside your body. Begin to notice the breath, the rise and fall of your breathing. How the breath moves in and out of the body. You may notice your chest or stomach rising and falling. Or the movement of the breath in the throat or nostrils."

3. Reader: "Keep your concentration on these physical sensations to the best of your ability."

4. Reader: "If thoughts arise, such as planning or memories, or if sensations arise, such as pain, tingling or numbness, gently let go of these thoughts and bring your attention back to the breath."

5. Note to Reader: You can repeat steps three and four every few minutes, or for ten, fifteen or thirty minutes.

Variation: Meditate with your partner, and synchronize your breathing.

Notes

There are many good CDs with instructions for basic meditation available from http://www.dharmaseed.org.

Dharma Seed operates on a donation basis, so you can try out different teachers quite inexpensively. Excellent teachers like Jack Kornfield, James Baraz, and Tara Brach have recorded talks and meditation instructions on that site.

APPENDIX 3
Form for Couples' Interlocking Patterns of Conflict (Practices Three and Five)

What was the first physical or emotional signal that you were beginning to feel stressed, distant or upset?

Did you go into a predicable pattern then?

Did you begin to feel anxious, angry or separate then?

What is the first thing you remember saying?

What was your tone of voice? Did you notice any changes in the way you were talking? (Louder, slower, quieter, more urgently?)

How did your breathing change when you went into your response?

What were your posture and body language?

What were they expressing?

What were they concealing?

Did you have tight or stressed body tensions? Where in your body did you feel these?

Did you notice any other body signals?

What was the most predominant feeling you had? (Examples: anger, sadness, or loneliness.)

Were there any more subtle feelings that might have been hard to notice?

How does this pattern of feelings and reactions that you just described seem familiar from other relationships? From seeing one of your parents or siblings act this way.

Have you had similar reactions before?

What can you learn about yourself from studying these reactions? Your history of relationship? Your parents' influence on you?

APPENDIX 4
Practices to Address Specific Couples' Problems

Problem: Busy-ness
Practice One: Being Present, or "Here I Am"

This Practice allows couples to settle down, to connect quietly, if you are too busy and disconnected.

Problem: Not Enough Positive Feelings Being Expressed
Practice Two: Appreciation–What Your Partner Deserves!

This Practice encourages couples to express their love and appreciation, and takes your attention off the many, many errands of running a household together.

Problem: Lack of Communication Skills
Practice Three: Communication Model 1–Can We Talk?

Most of us have never learned to reveal ourselves to our partner. This Practice begins teaching you how to communicate in an authentic way, the key to emotional connection.

Problem: The Relationship Drifting
Practice Four: Working with Intentions–Creating A Vision

Sometimes the relationship is stagnant and one of you is asking, "Why are we together?" This Practice helps you find a powerful motivation to remain committed: to heal and to grow.

Problem: Couples Cannot Talk to Each Other About Problems
Practice Five: Communications Model 2–I Didn't Know You Felt That

This Practice builds communication skills so you and your partner can talk about your repeating issues and conflicts with more openness and vulnerability.

Problem: Volatility and Fighting
Practice Six: Time-Out: Stop in the Name of Love and Return to Connection

This Practice enables you to de-escalate a conflict and to learn communication skills that lead to understanding and connection.

Problem: Power Struggles and Negative Thinking
Practice Seven: Creativity, Collaboration and Joy

This Practice supports mindfulness when you are working with your partner on planning and projects, and helps you be more creative.

Problem: Subtle Distance That Can Arise Between Partners
Practice Eight: Awareness of the Field–Is That You Over There?

This Practice builds awareness skills that can be used in the relationship.

Problem: Couples Getting Mired In the Mundane
Practice Nine: A Positive Connection–Creating More Love and Happiness

This Practice gives you ways to connect and build a positive, happy relationship.

Problem: Couples Not Knowing How the Relationship Could Work
Practice Ten: More Key Intentions

This Practice describes how to do creative play in the service of the relationship.

Acknowledgments & Gratitude

Loving Wife and Collaborator in Healing and Awakening: Debra Chamberlin Taylor.

Professional Allies and Consultants: Jon Leland, Katherine Dieter, Denise Minter.

Devoted and Inspirational Couples and Friends: Robert Adamich and Susan Shloss, Larry Tackett and Amrit Rai.

Incomparable Teachers: Tsoknye Rinpoche, Gay and Katie Hendricks, Jack Kornfield, Stephen and Ondrea Levine, Joanna Macy.

Professional Colleagues and Inspirations: James and Jane Baraz, Tara Brach, Rick Hanson, Linda Graham, Roger Housden, Judi Bell, Christine Carter.

Powerful Therapists and Heartful Thinkers: Ahria Wolf, Pearlyn Goodman-Herrick, Kim Rosen.

Great Therapists and Friends in the Men's Counseling Guild: Alan Ptashek, Russell Sutter, Gordon Clay, Erik Grabow, Lou Dangles, Gary Hoeber, Andrew Michaels, Daniel Ellenberg.

The Daos Brothers, Creative Forces and Community Servants: Dan Zola, Guillermo Ortiz, Doug Von Koss.

Incredibly Loyal and Supportive Family: William Taylor, Mary Robertson, Joseph Taylor and Linda Liebschutz, Teresa and Greg Paxton, Chris Paxton, Julia Paxton.

Extended Incredibly Loyal and Supportive Family: Ane and Marc Takaha, Clare McGlaughlin, Devi Weisenberg, Jo and Carolyn Hobbs, Helen Richfield and Rusty Hedlin.

Those Who Are No Longer With Us Who Loved Art and the Soul: Rosemary Taylor, Marr Taylor, Kathleen Taylor, Stan Weisenberg.

About the Author

George Taylor, a California licensed Marriage and Family Therapist, spent over thirty years trying to understand how to be an effective healer for couples. The Practices and ideas in this book come from his experience creating transformational workshops, groups and counseling sessions.

He is grateful for his training with brilliant couples therapists and spiritual teachers like Gay and Katie Hendricks and Steven and Ondrea Levine. These innovators have developed powerful teachings and practices that help their students learn how to use relationship as a path of transformation and healing.

His mindfulness teachers include Jack Kornfield and Tsoknyi Rinpoche. George has been married since 1981 to a powerful therapist and teacher, Debra Chamberlin Taylor. He is not sure if his professional training or his marriage to a powerful, thoughtful wife has

been more important for creating this book. He and Debra live and work in Marin County, California.

The Ten Practices come from his life's work creating healing workshops and programs for American couples with common stressors and communication problems. Please visit his website **www.pathforcouples.com** for information about online courses, counseling, and more writing.

NOTES

NOTES

NOTES

NOTES

Notes

NOTES

NOTES

NOTES

NOTES

CPSIA information can be obtained
at www.ICGtesting.com
Printed in the USA
FSHW012035141220
76901FS

9 780964 412910